GUIDE TO KNIFE & AXE THROWING

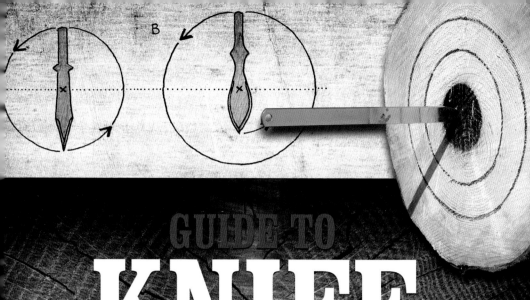

GUIDE TO
KNIFE
& AXE
THROWING

Dieter Führer

Schiffer
Publishing Ltd

4880 Lower Valley Road • Atglen, PA 19310

Type set in Bertold Akzidenz

ISBN: 978-0-7643-4779-5
Printed in China

Published by Schiffer Publishing, Ltd.
4880 Lower Valley Road
Atglen, PA 19310
Phone: (610) 593-1777; Fax: (610) 593-2002
E-mail: Info@schifferbooks.com

"wood background" © Vitaliy Pakhnyushchyy. "Dried tree cut texture" © Zibedik. Images from BigStockPhoto.com

For our complete selection of fine books on this and related subjects, please visit our website at www.schifferbooks.com. You may also write for a free catalog.

This book may be purchased from the publisher. Please try your bookstore first.

We are always looking for people to write books on new and related subjects. If you have an idea for a book, please contact us at proposals@schifferbooks.com.

Schiffer Publishing's titles are available at special discounts for bulk purchases for sales promotions or premiums. Special editions, including personalized covers, corporate imprints, and excerpts can be created in large quantities for special needs. For more information, contact the publisher.

Originally published as Handbuch Messer- und Axtwerfen by Wieland Verlag GmbH, Bad Aibling, Germany
© 2011 by Wieland Verlag GmbH
Author: Dieter Führer
Translated from the German by Ingrid Elser
Dr. John Guess, editorial advisor

CONTENTS

PREFACE

For a long time, I toyed with the idea of writing a guide to knife and axe throwing. Most books on the topic of knife throwing were published in the late 1980s and thus are no longer up-to-date and really need to be revised. And about axe throwing – with the exception of a short manual about throwing double axes translated from Swedish – nothing of relevance exists. These are good reasons for bringing something new to the market.

Sporting knife and axe throwing is presently experiencing an outright boom. Interest in it has increased enormously and led to the foundation of the European Society of Throwers, the "Flying Blades" (Eurothrowers) in the summer of 2003. This increasing interest has also been confirmed by the fact that manufacturers of steel products have offered an incredible variety of objects for throwing – difficult for beginners to choose from oftentimes.

Thus, I first turned to combing through the relevant literature. But I also assembled and tested more than a hundred different throwing objects – starting with the double axe and ending with the bo shuriken. In addition, I had the opportunity to talk with, exchange experiences, and measure my skills with those of like-minded people during countless meetings and throwing contests in Germany, as well as foreign countries.

This book is essentially based on my personal techniques and experience. But the knowledge of other distinguished throwers also contributes to this book: from practical experience for practical use.

Dieter Führer

PART A: KNIFE THROWING

Knife throwing – this you know from Hollywood movies, circus arenas, and the stages of variety shows. There, with a sure move, the hero takes out his enemy...or the artist throws sharp objects with breathtaking precision towards his attractive, scantily clad partner – thank God, without hitting her!

Knife throwing is not that easy to learn. It can be quite frustrating, especially at the beginning, due to the many throws that don't hit the target. It also has high demands with respect to the ability to concentrate, eye-hand coordination, and a feel for the movement. But when the blades finally fly the way you want them to, and reliably strike the target, you will be fascinated.

But as we know: no pain, no gain. Don't give up! It will turn out well!

SAFETY

"It is a bitter blade, and steel serves only those that can wield it. It will cut your hand as willingly as aught else."
–J.R.R. Tolkien: *The Children of Húrin*

Knife and axe throwing are surely not without dangers. Accordingly, everyone participating in this sport is obligated to behave in such a way as to prevent injury. The following safety precautions are under no circumstances to be neglected:

1. Never – not even suggestively! – aim towards humans or animals.
2. No one should be in the line of throwing or in the vicinity of the target.
3. The entire area around the line of throwing must be clearly visible.
4. The line of throwing has to be free of hindrances, such as low-hanging twigs.
5. All spectators must stay at a reasonable distance behind the thrower.
6. Always be aware that the thrown objects may bounce off or bounce backwards.
7. Underage persons are only allowed to throw under competent supervision by an experienced person.
8. Always keep the throwing knives in suitable sheaths, especially if you carry them on your body. Throwing axes should have their blade edges covered.
9. The background should be of a kind that thrown objects can't get lost if you miss the target.
10. Don't abuse living trees by using them as targets!

If several throwers are throwing at the same time – which almost always happens during meetings and contests – there have to be agreements with respect to walking towards the target and retrieving the thrown objects. It is recommended that a person should be designated responsible for checking the safety issues, especially during training and warming up – all the more if the throwing trajectories are close to each other.

Definition of Parts:
Throwing Knife With Sheath

To avoid misunderstandings, here you find the most important expressions with respect to throwing knives.

The European competition rules require a minimum overall length of 9 inches (23 centimeters) and a maximum blade width of about 2 inches (5 centimeters).

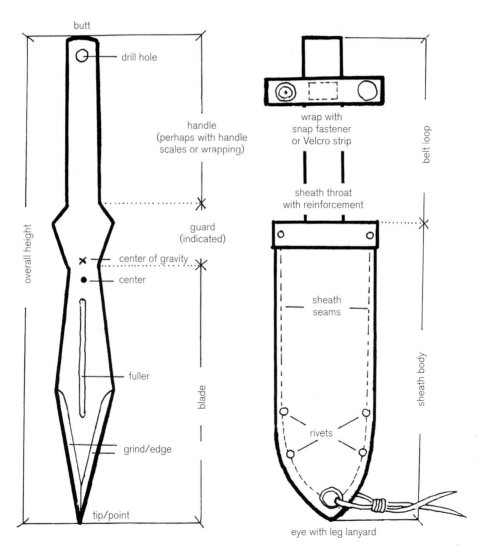

PREPARATIONS

So, you are really determined to learn how to throw knives? Then let's start from scratch. If you know somebody who is already proficient, you can let him/her teach you. But if you want to learn it without help from anyone else, you'd best follow the path described in this book.

Constructing a Steel Blade for Throwing

Unless you already have a certain proficiency in throwing knives, you don't have to spend money to buy a throwing knife. Otherwise, the possibility is quite high that you'll invest in a type that you might regret. There are numerous variants that, in part, differ considerably from each other. You can't know yet which one is the right one for you. So, for the beginning, a steel blade that you make yourself is sufficient.

If you already own a throwing knife that is at least approximately 10 inches (25 centimeters) in length, weighs about 9 ounces (250 grams) and has a straight handle, then, of course, you can use this instead of the handmade steel piece for throwing.

For your own throwing knife, first of all, you will need to obtain a piece of steel sheet or strip steel. Things like this can be found at a junk yard or between the pieces of trash in a locksmith's shop. It ought to be about 13 inches (35 centimeters) in length, about an inch (2.5 to 3 centimeters) in width and have a thickness of just under two tenths of an inch (4-5 millimeters).

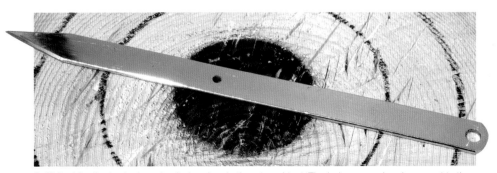

Sufficient for the beginning: simple, handmade throwing object. The holes were already present in the source material and have no function.

The end of this piece is sharpened to a solid tip by means of a grinding block. The grind doesn't necessarily have to be sharp, but the point should be. Now, the edges of the longitudinal sides and the butt have to be rounded ("broken") with a file and your throwing knife is finished.

For the beginning, this is absolutely sufficient and surely less expensive than buying a similar throwing knife. Maybe you can even make a set of three pieces. If you can't or don't want to do the necessary work yourself, any locksmith can do it for you.

Making or Finding a Target

The next thing, of course, is finding a solid target. Naturally, you never will – and I repeat: *never!* – throw at living trees. This is prohibited, as nature should be respected. Besides, you can easily create suitable targets for knives and axes yourself with only little effort, as well as find them afield or in the forest.

Propped-up Tree Disc

Tree discs are waste parts of the wood. You can obtain them at saw mills. Best are those from the end of a fir log. The diameter should be around 19 inches (50 centimeters); the thickness should measure at least 8 inches (20 centimeters). The thicker, the better, because tree discs rupture easily when drying out. You can prevent this by watering them every once in a while.

You drill three blind holes with a diameter of a little over 2 inches (6 centimeters) each into this tree disc. Into these, hammer the stilts (with the same diameter and each about 5 feet [1.5 meters] in length) onto which the tree disc is propped. Larger and heavier pieces can also be placed upon a tripod made of square timbers (construction manual on page 101). Tree discs can also be hung on a wall. In this case, you should first attach a lining of planks to catch misses. You also have to consider that your throws create noise when hitting. Accordingly, be respectful of others.

Target variants: tree section propped on three stilts or on a tripod of three square timbers.

Can be found in the forest: stacked tree logs.

Pyramid of Tree Logs

The depicted tree log pyramid was erected in a forest clearing and enables the constant change of targets while throwing. The logs (waste wood from trees infested with disease) were fixed on the backside with cramp irons and have been used as throwing targets for more than ten years already.

Stake

A tree trunk of about 6 ½ feet (2 meters) in length with a minimal diameter of about 12 inches (30 centimeters) is embedded in the ground. It is cut with a chain saw in such a way that a flat surface is created, which you can use as a target. This cut makes hitting the target easier because otherwise you would have to hit the trunk, more or less, at its center.

Throwing Wall Made of Glued Square Timbers

The depicted wall with the dimensions 78 x 29 x 6½ inches (200 x 75 x 17 centimeters) is quite heavy and can barely be carried by

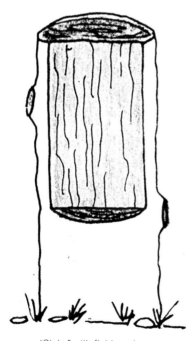

"Stake" with flat target area.

Elaborate construction and high weight: throwing wall of square timbers.

two people. It is stabilized by two supports at the backside. Its construction takes a lot of effort, but the throwing wall shown here has been on duty for ten years already and can withstand the roughest conditions. If the front side is tattered, the wall is turned around.

Tree Log Tilted at an Angle

Such simple targets can easily be created from waste wood left over in the forest after harvesting. In order to tilt the stump at the desired angle, either round timbers can be put underneath or a log is used as a base. Ask the property owner for his/her permission, to be on the safe side.

Simple solutions: the faces of tilted tree logs.

Natural Targets

These are frequently created by storm-damaged trees and debris that has been dealt with afterwards. The cut surfaces, in this case, provide especially attractive targets that don't require any effort. But here, too, you had better ask for permission first.

Additional Tips

And what else has to be considered? Fir wood is well suited as material for constructing targets. This is the case for all coniferous wood, but also for soft wood from deciduous trees, e.g. poplar or basswood. In any case, tree discs are preferred over planks or boards.

As if made for knife throwing: "natural" targets found by chance.

When constructing a target, you always have to consider the grain of the wood, so your throwing object can penetrate easily and become reliably stuck. Of course, the front side of the target has to be free of metal parts (nails, screws, wire, etc.). Abstain from using hardwood because it impairs the penetration of the blade. The same goes for resinous wood, because otherwise the sticky stuff will be found again on your throwing objects, as well as your hands. (This is an especially unpleasant feeling – not only before, but during throwing.)

The target is always marked with at least one center ("bull's eye") – for example a colored dot, a leaf, or a playing card – at which you aim and should be able to hit. This way, you also enhance your ability to concentrate and thus your accuracy in hitting the target. Of course, you can also affix several "bull's eyes," since changing the target frequently helps to improve accuracy.

If the ground in proximity to the target – especially right in front of it – is hard (concrete, rocks, asphalt, etc.), cover it with mats, pieces of carpet, or chipboard in order to prevent damage of the thrown objects when missing the target.

Finally, you should also take into account that your throws create noise when hitting – even more so when missing. Accordingly, be respectful of people who may live nearby.

INITIAL TRAINING
(Throwing from the Shortest Distance and Without Rotation*)

Handle and Handling

After the object to throw and the target have been created, it is finally time to start throwing. Here you can see how to best hold the throwing knife:

Hold it as if you were holding a hammer, while aligning it approximately parallel to the ground. The thumb rests on the back of the throwing knife. The little finger just barely touches the end. Don't hold on too hard; hold the knife rather lightly!

Standard grip: the throwing knife is held like a hammer.

*The following descriptions are all made for right-handed persons. Left-handed persons follow the instructions with adaptation.

Stance and Aiming

You stand in front of the target this way:

Stand as if about to lunge. The foot in front
– for a right-handed person, this is always the
left foot! – with a distance to the target of
approximately 6 feet (1.5 meters). The rear foot
is about one step behind.

Your right shoulder is exactly opposite the
target, which means that the central axis of your
body is slightly off the center of the target.

The weight of your body distinctly rests on the
foot in front. Because of this, your left knee is
slightly bent. The lateral distance between both
feet is approximately the width of your
shoulders. The sketch shows the stance from
above.

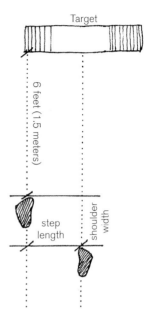

Start of the initial training: taking measure at a distance of 1.5 meters to the target.

If you are standing with the feet too close together, your balance is unstable. If your feet are too far apart, your stance will become cramped. Admittedly, my stance on the photos is rather wide. But this is always the case with me and may be a result of my past as a budo athlete.

Your free hand is put flat on your abdomen. There it stays, because there you have it under control. You can also put the hand on your groin or thigh, behind your back, or into the pocket of your trousers. It should always be at the same place with every throw in order to avoid uncontrolled movements that could influence your balance in an unwanted way.

Now, you lift your hand with the throwing knife until its tip points towards the center of the target. Upper arm, lower arm, hand, and throwing knife are more or less lined up. This phase is called "taking measure."

Is your upper torso upright and your head straight? Fix your eyes on the center of the target: you focus on the upcoming throw!

Bring Your Arm Back, Throw and Follow Through

Now, lift the knife hand to above the height of your head while, at the same time, bending your arm for throwing in such a way that the upper arm is adjusted horizontally and your forearm vertically. The tip of the throwing knife now faces upwards. Your wrist can be slightly flexed.

From this position, swing your throwing arm forward and downward with a powerful, circular movement. Your right shoulder follows this forward and downward movement and takes your upper torso with it.

Now follows the most difficult moment: letting go! There is no authoritative recommendation with respect to the when and where of letting go. Sometimes it is said that you ought to let go at the very moment the tip of the knife faces the target. This is wrong in any case, because this definitely has to be done earlier – at about the height of your crown! The sketch on page 23 reveals why this is the case.

Bringing your arm back: the arm is lifted, slightly turned toward the outside and bent.

The same seen from behind: the throwing knife points upwards/backwards, the elbow points to the outside.

Ready position: here, the throwing knife is far back, the body moves forward already.

Surely you'll get a feel for this after a couple of tries and will instinctively do it the right way. A crumpled piece of paper, as well, almost naturally finds its way from your hand to the waste paper basket, describing a trajectory through the air over a distance of about 12 feet (3 meters) by means of your hand-eye coordination.

Did you ever even think beforehand exactly when the paper has to leave your hand and how much force you have to apply? No, because your body has already adjusted itself to tasks like this a long time ago and thus functions "instinctively."

It only gets difficult if you've never tried to throw a stone, stick, or ball towards a target. But we'd better not take this as a premise.

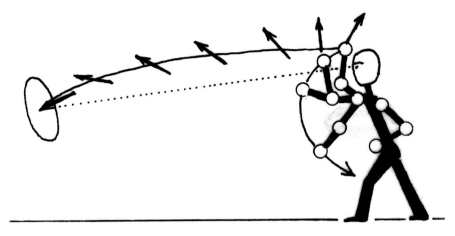

Schematically: the knife is already released when the tip faces upwards.

Automatically at the right moment: the movement just prior to the release of the knife.

Since you didn't hold the throwing knife too firmly, it will leave your hand as if of its own volition and will fly directly towards the target with its tip pointing at it. The knife doesn't rotate around its own axis – which would happen inevitably on a longer trajectory – because its tip is already sticking in the target before the rotation is complete.

The hit causes a rich, unique sound: *tchock!*

Under no circumstances should you stop the movement of your throwing arm right now and leave the arm suspended in the air, but continue the move in a circular arc until your hand has reached your left knee. Here, it can finally rest. We call this movement "follow through." In this stance, you should stay for a short moment; then you can straighten up.

You should never forego this act of following through, because you will not be able to achieve a consistently uniform motion sequence without it. This is essential for knife and axe throwing.

Now you may ask yourself: "But what if the knife ricochets after a miss while I am standing close enough in front of the target for it to hit me? Isn't this dangerous?"

Of course, this objection is reasonable. You always have to be aware that rebounds may occur. Your best possible protection: focus entirely on the throw. This also means that you always have to be prepared to dodge a rebound. In addition: the more diffidently you get down to business, the more frequently you will create rebounds!

This is how it should look: the thrown object hits the target; the throwing arm continues its movement.

Final position: the throwing arm rests on, or slightly in front of, the knee – stay in this position for a moment.

Corrections

If the throwing knife sticks in the wooden target at an angle, you should apply corrections. If the handle is facing downwards ("underwound") then:

- Extend the distance to the target by taking back the front foot a little bit (but by no more than the length of your foot!), or
- Let the throwing knife leave your hand a tad of a second earlier, or
- Hold the knife a bit more loosely.

If the handle faces upwards ("overwound"), you can either:

- Step a bit closer towards the target, or
- Let go of the throwing knife a bit earlier, or
- Grip the knife harder, or
- "Lean into the throw" a bit more, i.e., bend your upper torso forward a bit more.

The handle faces upwards: here, the throw is called overwound.

Handle facing downwards: such a throw is underwound.

Ideal case: the thrown object sticks straight in the target. The rotation fits exactly with the distance.

It should look just like this! If the throwing knife sticks in the target as in the photo above, you did everything right.

"Locked" Wrist

During each throw, you have to "lock" your wrist. This means your wrist should not be flexed or loose at the moment you let go of the knife. Your forearm, upper side of your thumb, and the throwing knife should form a straight line approximately.

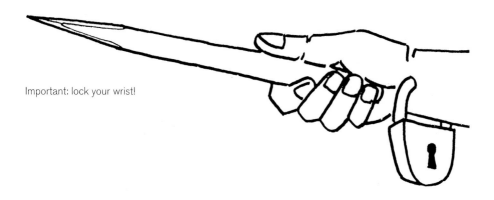

Important: lock your wrist!

Maybe the image will be helpful, showing that the knife is not really thrown, but flung.

Try, Try, Try Again!

The sketch on page 24 once more shows schematically what you have learned up to now: you see the motion sequence, the individual phases, and the trajectory of the thrown object.

Bear in mind that the thrown object is almost upright at the moment it leaves your hand and the trajectory is by no means straight, but has the shape of a ballistic curve. This curve is determined by the speed, the terrestrial pull (gravity), and the aerodynamic drag that act upon the object during flight.

And now we start practice! You should reenact the whole procedure while fully focusing on it until 25 out of 25 throws indeed hit the target. With continued practice, the motion sequence, which always stays the same, will become "ingrained" as your second nature.

After a while, you will realize that your throwing knife hits the target when you focus on it with your eyes, more and more often – within the range of ½ inch (1 centimeter)! If this is the case, you can move on to the next exercise.

BASIC THROW
Throwing From 13 Feet (4 Meters) with One Rotation

As a next step, you will train in throwing from a distance of 13 feet (4 meters) and with one full rotation. This we christened "basic throw" because it is the basis for all the different knife throws from various distances – regardless if it is 16 feet (5 meters), 23 feet (about 7 meters), or even farther away.

It won't be difficult for you to master the basic throw because you are already proficient in throwing over a short distance without rotation. The motion sequence during the basic throw is exactly the same. But now, the one foot in front is at a distance of about 13 feet (4 meters) away from the target, which means the object to be thrown rotates on its way to the target almost one and a quarter times – about 400°.

Frozen in time: the throwing knife at about the apex of its trajectory.

In no case can you "force" the rotation to happen by trying to give the thrown object an additional momentum with your hand or forearm. The throwing knife will rotate on its own. This is already assured by the circular movement of your throwing arm swinging downwards. Even if you would like to, you would not be able to stop the rotation.

Watch the tip of the blade each time you throw it. If the throwing knife rebounds without sticking in the target, and the blade tip faces downwards, the throw was overwound because you were standing too far off the target. In this case, shorten the distance by stepping forward about the length of one foot and try again.

But, in case the tip of the blade faces upwards during the rebound, the throw is underwound. Logically, you then have to step back a bit in order to increase the distance. You can experiment in order to find your optimal distance for the basic throw.

Of course, this procedure only works well when your motion sequence stays the same with every throw. There is a possibility for making lots of mistakes without realizing them immediately. Check time and again or let somebody else watch you.

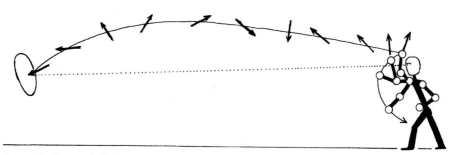

Schematic diagram: ballistic trajectory with one and a quarter rotations.

Especially important: The thrown object should always leave your hand at the same point and with the same velocity!

Rotational Velocities

Until now, you held the throwing knife the same way as shown on page 19. At the instant of letting go, a small torque is added by means of the slight pressure applied by your thumb on the blade's back. It acts against the rotation and slows it down.

Every once in a while, the thrown knife ricochets with the tip facing upwards, or it is stuck in the target in such a way that the handle faces the ground at a very acute angle. Increase the throwing distance a bit in order for the knife to stick well in the target once again.

You can also change your grip. It should look like the one shown on the next page at the bottom. Then the above described torque is gone and the throwing knife rotates a bit faster.

In contrast to this, the rotational speed is slowed down if your grip is somewhat more firm, because then the thrown knife has to overcome a higher frictional resistance while gliding off your hand. The same effect can be achieved when wrapping the handle with tape.

But in case your hands and/or the throwing knife are wet, it glides even faster from your hands than it usually does. This effect is an unwanted one that you should try to avoid. Thus, have a piece of cloth with you for drying, if the need arises.

Under no circumstances should you apply several changes at the same time to your throwing technique. This means, either you increase or decrease the distance or you change your grip – never do both at once!

Just for the sake of completeness: very experienced throwers can give their knives additional rotational speed while throwing with the wrist more relaxed. This way, for example, it is possible to throw a knife from a distance of 16 feet (5 meters) right into the target with either one or two rotations.

Classic grip: the thumb on top of the handle slows the rotation down a tad.

Alternative: with the thumb at the side, the throwing object rotates a bit faster.

Throws from Varying Distances

Of course, you won't always want to train for the basic throw from a distance of 13 feet (4 meters). If you have already mastered this, you can try throws from other distances: 10 feet (about 3 meters), 16 feet (about 5 meters), 23 feet (about 7 meters) are common at international contests. These distances are for orientation – this is done by most knife throwers.

The table further down shows how the distance and number of rotations are related to each other, depending on whether you want to do a throw with slow or fast rotation.

If you can cope with these parameters, you will also succeed in throws from larger distances by means of the principle "trial and error." The table, of course, can only serve as a reference. It should help you to develop your own, personal throwing style. Whether you are successful with this depends mainly on a consistently uniform and clean motion sequence.

The table also shows whether you should grip the knife at its handle or at the blade. Gripping the blade is quite common. Thus, as an example, we used the photo series on the next pages to illustrate the motion sequence once more: this time for throwing from a distance of about 16 feet (5 meters) with one and a half rotations and gripping the blade.

TABLE: DISTANCE, ROTATION, AND GRIP				
Distance	Number of rotations for		Grip for	
	slow rotation	fast rotation	slow rotation	fast rotation
10 feet (about 3 m)	½	1	Blade	Handle
13 feet (about 4 m)	1	1½	Handle	Blade
16 feet (about 5 m)	1½	2	Blade	Handle
23 feet (about 7 m)	2	3	Handle	Handle

Bringing the arm back: your throwing hand is lifted high above your head. During this, the elbow moves right to the outside; the throwing arm is bent.

Throw: the throwing hand is swung forward in a circle around the shoulder. The right shoulder follows this forward movement; the upper torso leans "into the throw".

Letting go: the knife is released at the height of your head and with the wrist locked. The throwing arm is outstretched at this time.

Following through: the throwing arm's movement is continued towards the left knee. Your eyes still focus on the target.

Following through: while you watch the knife hitting the target, the throwing hand rests open and relaxed on the left knee.

Choosing a Throwing Knife

Until now, you have managed quite well with your throwing object, but I imagine that you finally want to get a real throwing knife. Maybe you have already taken a look at what can be found on the market and realized that many manufacturers offer a multitude of throwing knives in various shapes and sizes. Which model is the one best suited? The following tips hopefully will make the choice easier for you.

First of all, the throwing knife has to be robust and almost indestructible because it has to endure a lot of hard treatment. It should also be able to survive misses without damage, if possible. These qualities can be found above all in throwing knives made from a single piece of flat steel that was shaped and finished.

But, of course, such a knife will eventually receive scratches and dents; it will lose its tip or even break. Therefore, the used steel should not be too hard or brittle. With a soft material, dents or a damaged blade can be corrected easily by means of hammer blows, and the blade can be smoothed with a file.

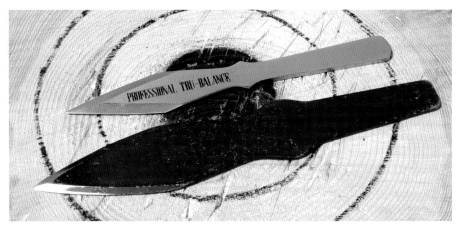

Simple, but good: throwing knives from a single piece of sheet steel.

Thus, often used throwing knives in general look quite battered. Accordingly, your tools don't necessarily have to be hardened to a high degree, be stainless or have a coating.

Surely, it is also useful to purchase a set of three throwing knives. In case the first throw is a miss, you then can immediately apply corrections during the second and third throws without having to fetch back a single knife first and set up your stance once again in front of the target.

Asymmetrical shapes, as well as cutouts and corners in the outline of a throwing knife, are seen as sales promoting by the manufacturers. But this should be looked at critically because they impede letting go without torque during the throw. This means your fingers may get caught on these cutouts and corners when letting go of the knife and thus add an unwanted momentum to its trajectory. Cut-outs, drill holes, and grooves are also unnecessary. They only help with accumulating dirt. Besides that, they bring down the weight, which for many knives is not a desired quality. But these considerations apparently are totally alien to many manufacturers.

Don't get taken in: the knife on top looks fancy, but the one below is definitely better suited for throwing.

Frailer than knives made of a single steel piece, in any case, are knives which are provided with handles riveted or screwed on by the manufacturer. These can crack very quickly or become loose, if they are not made of carefully attached and very robust material. Of course, this is also a question of cost. In case the handle scales are screwed on, you can loosen the screws and remove the handle scales in order to preserve them. If necessary, damaged handle scales are simply wrapped with tape.

Some models of throwing knives are wrapped with lanyard or paracord. They enhance the grip in any case and you can also easily replace them if they are damaged.

Of course, your knife should also have a sheath so you can stow it away safe and secure and – in case of need – also carry it on your body.

If the throwing knife is meant for all-round use, as a tool for multiple tasks, and thus was delivered with a sharp edge, you ought to blunt it with a file or at least cover it with tape to avoid inadvertent injuries. The tip, however, should really be pointed, because it ought to "bite" well even with hard wood.

If the models are advertised with qualities such as "perfectly balanced," "unerring," or "professionally designed stainless throwing knife for artists," you may allow yourself to be skeptical. Even highly praised (and accordingly very expensive) knives require a sophisticated throwing technique and don't guarantee perfect throws of their own volition. Even the best piece of sports equipment is only as good as the sportsperson using it.

If you buy at a retail store, a mail-order business, or via the Internet, unfortunately you are not able to test the knife of your choice. But maybe you'll have the opportunity to attend a meeting of throwers and buy a knife there. This you can test right then. But if immediate testing is not possible, take the throwing knife you like best, that has all the required qualities, into your hand. Hold it at the handle, as if you were about to throw it; hold it at its blade. Does it feel comfortable? If this is the case, take it!

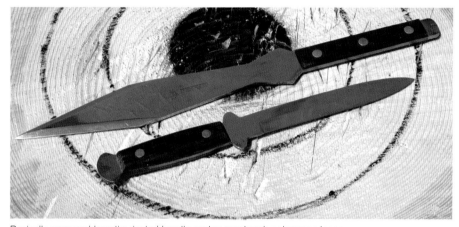

Basically more problematic: riveted handle scales may break or become loose.

Better solution: lanyard wraps as handle material are robust and can easily be replaced.

THE RIGHT BALANCE

The Center of Gravity

Somehow, the idea seems to have affixed itself in people's minds that a throwing knife has to be "perfectly balanced" to be suitable. This probably means that the center of gravity has to be exactly at the center of its overall length. Correct! Then, of course, it will rotate around this point on its way to the target. The radius of this rotation in this case is equivalent to half the knife's length. Result: uniform rotations, regardless of throwing the knife by its blade or the handle. This, in any case, is an advantage and can be seen below in image A.

A knife of equal length whose center of gravity is about a third of its length, in contrast, will have a rotation with a distinctly larger radius. This is shown in image B. Despite the imbalance, this knife is suited well, too, for throwing. For larger distances, it is even more advantageous, because the knife rotates fewer times over the same distance.

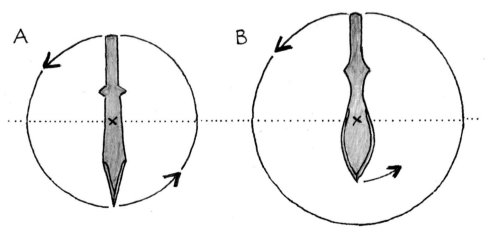

Rotational circle: if the center of gravity is outside the knife's center, the radius is larger for the same knife length.

In general, the following is valid: fewer rotations mean more control because of fewer sources of error. The small aberrations, which you can hardly avoid during the release, don't make themselves obvious over a short distance. But for increased throwing distances, they "build up" with every rotation and eventually can spoil your throw.

If you take a knife into your hand for throwing ("taking aim"), the center of gravity, with the throwing arm outstretched, should be in front of your hand. In general, you can thus initially apply the following rule of thumb:

Center of gravity in the handle→grip the blade
Center of gravity in the blade→grip the handle

If you are not sure of your knife's center of gravity, you can balance it on your outstretched forefinger.

Searching for the center of gravity: the knife is balanced on the outstretched finger.

Adjustable Weights

"A throwing knife with two adjusting screws should enable you to adjust the knife to your individual throwing technique, for every throw to become a success." This is the text in the catalog in which the supplier advertises the left of the three shown throwing knives below. But how this is supposed to work is not explained further for this product from the Far East. The potential customer is given an impression of something utterly impossible.

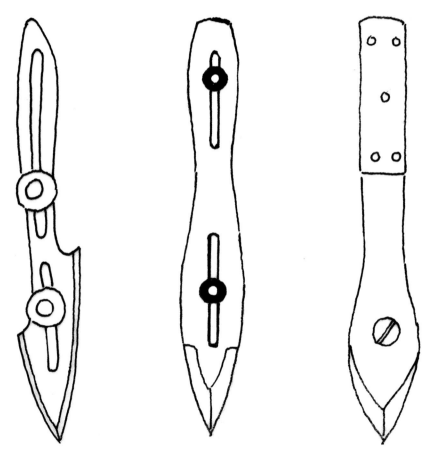

Of doubtful use: throwing knives with movable weights or screws whose weight is too small to effectively influence the center of gravity.

This asymmetrical throwing knife has two slits in its longitudinal axis in which two weights of .028 ounces (8 grams) each are held by means of Allen screws. When the screws are loosened, the weights can be slid and fixed again at any place. But, the throwing knife's center of gravity without the weight lies exactly in the center – just the way it should be. Regardless of where the weights are placed, the center of gravity is only moved by a couple of millimeters, because the balancing weights only weigh .028 ounces (8 grams) – a factor that surely has theoretical but hardly any practical effects.

The same goes for the symmetrical throwing knife of the same length shown in the center. Its balancing weights have a mass of .021 ounces (6 grams) each. With this knife, too, the center of gravity can only be moved by a couple of millimeters – which gives no advantage.

The right knife, in contrast, is a real curiosity: it stems from a renowned manufacturer in Solingen, Germany, and has only one slotted screw of .028 ounces (8 grams) weight, which is held in place by an internal screw thread within the first one-third of the blade. Tightening as well as loosening the screw are supposed to influence the center of gravity and thus to adjust the throwing knife to the hand. Actually, this is hardly comprehensible, all the more considering the knife's weight of 11 ounces (320 grams). Nevertheless, these pieces of the 1960s are sought-after collector items today.

These balancing weights, by the way, slip easily or get lost when they become detached. Such things should be seen as mere decoration, which fail that designated duty. Thus, you can forego them without regrets.

Ultimately the following is valid:
A throwing knife is not adjusted to the thrower and his/her style in throwing, but the thrower has to recognize the qualities of the knife and adjust to them.

Length and Weight

Let's assume that, after some amount of training with your throwing knife, you want to participate in a contest, the main goal being to hit a round target as exactly as possible in the center and to gain points by doing so – just to meet other throwers and to find out where you stand compared to them.

In this case, it makes no sense to show up with a toy, such as the one illustrated in the drawing below. The original of this little knife, at a length of about 6 inches (15.5 centimeters), has a weight of nearly 2 ounces (55 grams). It may be just sufficient for playful throws from a distance of about 10 feet (3 meters). But this is hardly the case for throws from a distance of 16 or more feet (5 or more meters) during a sporting contest. In this case, you would have to throw it very powerfully in order for it to achieve the necessary velocity to penetrate deep enough in the wood and to stick in the target reliably. Also, constant throwing with all your power in the long run overstresses the muscles of your arms and shoulders. This can be very painful for somebody who throws a lot.

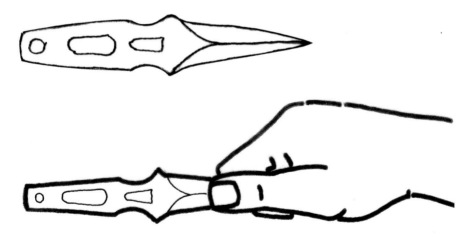

Not a good throwing knife: the original of the depicted dagger is too short and lightweight.

Besides this, you already know from the previous pages of this chapter that a knife of short length during flight inevitably makes a lot of rotations over a given distance, which, in addition, are relatively quick. In connection with the low weight, at a distance of about 16 feet (5 meters) already, an unstable momentum is created called "flutter." This is the case all the more so if the knife is gripped as shown in the drawing, because then, the rotations are accelerated even more. Clean hits under these circumstances occur rather by chance.

You surely want to have the feeling that something really "weighty" is flung from your hand towards the target – which was already the case with your handmade throwing object. Where else should the pronounced *tchok!* stem from as the blade dives into the wood and which all throwers rave about?

Length does the job: longer and heavier throwing knives are easier to throw than short, light ones.

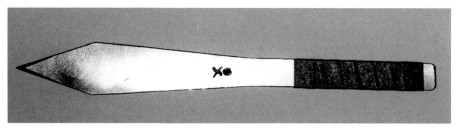

A real monster: this throwing knife has a length of nearly 15 inches (38 centimeters), a thickness of six millimeters, and weighs more than 17 ounces (500 grams). Half its length (dot) and center of gravity (X) almost coincide.

Since length and weight are dependent on each other, I urgently recommend a throwing knife of at least 10 inches (25 centimeters) length with a blade thickness of about a sixth of an inch (4 or 5 millimeters). You should not settle for anything less. If this has a weight of about 8 ounces (250 grams), too, you have made the right choice. From this follows another rule of thumb:

Weight in grams = length in centimeters x 10

Most of the commercially produced throwing knives only roughly approximate this ratio. But here, a difference of about 1.5 ounces (50 grams) literally "doesn't carry weight." However, with lighter or much heavier types, there is quite often a strong discrepancy.

Big knives, because of their inertia resulting from their high weight, are forgiving with respect to small mistakes of the thrower, but, in turn, demand lots of force for the throw. In general, the following is valid:

A long and heavy throwing knife is easier to control than a short and light one.

TYPES OF THROWING KNIVES

Throwing Knife Classics

Such elaborately worked throwing knives as shown on this page were produced by renowned manufacturers at Solingen during the 1950s and '60s. Partially, these blades are even "tapered," which in this case means the material thickness increases towards the tip. The handles are made of stacked leather rings with intersecting layers of vulcanized fiber. But the third knife from the right already has a handle of plastic.

Harry K. McEvoy from Grand Rapids, Michigan (who died in 1993) founded the Tru-Balance Knife Company in 1949, producing high-quality throwing knives, three of which are shown on page 49. He was also the

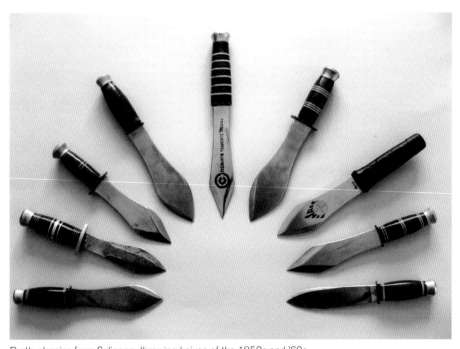

Pretty classics from Solingen: throwing knives of the 1950s and '60s.

founder of the American Knife Throwers Alliance (AKTA) and published several books and papers on the topic of knife and tomahawk throwing (see Bibliography).

Throwing knives of the legendary Tru-Balance Knife Company:
1. "Bowie Axe" (length 13 inches [34 centimeters], weight 14½ ounces [415 grams])
2. "Professional" (13 inches, 8 ounces [34 centimeters, 235 grams])
3. "Heavyweight Sport-Pro" (13 inches, 14½ ounces [34 centimeters, 410 grams])

Special Types of Throwing Knives

Flying Knife

This unusual throwing knife was designed by the Spaniard Paco Tovar. It measures about 12 inches (32 centimeters) in length, weighs about 7½ ounces (215 grams), and consists of a small, but sturdy blade (a fifth of an inch or 5 mm in thickness) and a cylindrical handle with an opening close to its lower end. While the throwing hand holds the knife in a way similar to a spear or dart, the forefinger is stuck into a hole. During the throw, the forefinger should transfer that momentum to the knife, which makes it rotate around its longitudinal axis in a stabilized way without doing somersaults. Thus, it always flies tip forward and is supposed to make throws over long distances easier. On the other hand, this technique is not easy to master, even for experienced throwers.

Totally different: the Flying Knife is held like a spear with the forefinger in the opening.

Starlight

This special design (length about 11 inches, weight about 1 ounce [28 centimeters, weight 318 grams]) of John Bailey can be provided with optical or acoustical effects. A cut out in the blade's center can hold a small fluorescent tube by means of which the trajectory of the knife can be followed in the darkness. The fluorescent tube can be replaced by a striker to detonate a percussion cap similar to that in a child's cap gun on impact.

Hungarian Commando Knife

This robust tactical and utility knife is a military design and development made in Hungary. Its blade is sharpened on one side and its handle is ergonomically shaped from natural rubber. The knife is delivered with an elaborately finished leather sheath, with an inner protection for the blade edge made of sheet steel. The sheath is connected to its mounting by means of a plug connection and can be easily disconnected from it by pressing a lock with a spring mechanism. When aiming for a throw, the knife is inside the sheath and thus not touched by the thrower's hand. By the movement of throwing, it is flung out of the sheath and towards the target. But the knife has to be loosened inside the sheath prior to the throw. The frictional resistance during the release from the sheath varies with each throw and makes the throws unpredictable.

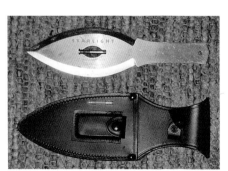

With built-in extras: Starlight throwing knife with fluorescent tube or percussion cap in the blade.

Unusual idea: the Hungarian commando knife can be flung from its sheath, but this doesn't work really well.

MILITARY STYLE KNIFE THROWING

The Requirements

Worldwide, the members of armed and security forces – especially special units – are provided with so-called "tactical knives." Their shapes and layouts vary greatly and depend on their intended use. The legendary fame of some well-known models quite often has no relation to their usability in the field. But they nevertheless are of importance to their users as a symbol of status.

A useful tactical knife has to be designed to be a utility knife first because it will be used as a weapon only under very rare circumstances. Knife throwing as a possible type of application in the tactical realm will not be discussed here.

Tactical-style fixed blades: Bowie knife in black, Ka-Bar USMC, a modified Glock field knife, and the combat knife KM 2000 of the company Eickhorn, Solingen.

Nevertheless, it is a fact that many tactical knives are quite suited as throwing knives, but in case the butt of the knife is very pronounced and strongly profiled – as is the case with several models – the knife can't leave the hand of the thrower cleanly. This means it is hard to throw them successfully when gripping the handle. Another problem, in general, is the center of gravity lies inside the handle. Gripping the blade is thus the obvious choice.

However, the blade edge is ground to be very sharp in order to do its task. A thrower can easily be injured. Thus, the most important advice is: keep your fingers away from the sharp edge! "Military-style throwing" was developed as a result of these special requirements.

Conducting the Throws

Take a stance like the one for the basic throw – the front foot at a distance of just over 10 feet (3 meters) to the target. You grip the knife the same way as is shown on the following page.

The thumb of the throwing hand rests flat on the blade. The fingers hold the blade in such a way that the blunt blade back rests in the palm of your hand. The sharp edge pokes out between your fingers and is not touched.

While taking aim, the blade is held horizontally, parallel to the ground – the thumb has to be on top! Let the blade slide from your hand during the throw. On its way to the target, it will do slightly more than half a rotation. Look at the blade's tip during impact. If it faces upwards, you have to increase the distance a tiny bit.

During the throw from a distance of about 13 feet (4 meters), the half rotation stays the same. But to adjust to the longer distance, the grip of the blade has to be changed slightly. It then looks the same as on page 55 top photo:

Careful, sharp: the knife is held by its blade in such a way that the sharp edge lies lateral between the fingers and is not touched.

Your hand grips the blade in such a way that your thumb tip touches the bottom of the guard. Everything else stays the same as before. While throwing, let the blade glide through your hand over its entire length!

With the throw from a distance of about 16 feet (5 meters), the rotation will still be a half one. But again, you have to change your grip at the blade. This time it is in the following way:

Now your forefinger rests on the blade and its tip touches the bottom of the guard. In addition, apply a strong pressure to the blade's heel at the instant of letting go. Here the idea may be helpful to pushing the knife towards the target. This appears to be more complicated than it really is. But, of course, it doesn't work from scratch and has to be trained well.

If a knife is thrown with all a person's strength, it is entirely possible for it to achieve a velocity of up to about 37 miles per hour (60 kilometers per hour) during its flight. With this velocity, it then horizontally penetrates the wood. The forces which occur during the sudden stop of the rotation are extremely stressful for the blade. Every now and then a blade cracks under these lateral loads. The knife handle, too, can be irreversibly damaged during misses. Thus, you should ask yourself beforehand whether you really want to stress your original Ka-Bar knife this much.

Grip for throw from a distance of 13 feet (4 meters): the thumb now rests at the handle's front end.

Grip for throw from a distance of 16 feet (5 meters): the forefinger rests on the blade's side.

ALTERNATIVE GRIP TYPES

Throwing from the Flat Han

Besides the already described possibilities, you can also hold the knife for throwing perpendicular to the ground with the hand held flat. Here, the thumb presses the blade against the palm of your hand. This looks like the photo below.

This is not a very stable position for the knife. Therefore, the centrifugal force of the arc-like forward and downward movement of your throwing arm will pull the knife off your hand almost automatically. Light knives (up to 8-9 ounces [about 250 grams]) are well suited for this. The difficulty with this technique is to dose the pressure of your thumb against the knife to be about the same with each throw. Otherwise, the knife will either leave your hand too early – which results in a high throw – or too late (result: a low throw). Of course, the wrist has to be locked.

The photo shows the grip for a throw with half a rotation. For throws with full rotations, the handle of the knife has to lie in the palm of your hand.

Alternative grip: the blade is held between thumb and palm.

Underhand Throw

This method of grip is well-suited for another technique – the underhand throw. Grip the knife in your hand as just described. Hold your hand next to your thigh in such a way that the flat side of the blade is oriented towards the target. Then you take aim backwards, swing the arm forward, and let the knife glide off your hand with the outstretched arm at about the height of your hip. Over a distance of about 10 feet (3 meters) it will turn about 180° against the direction of throwing. This is shown in the sketch below.

Actually, this technique is not recommended because, due to its low acceleration, the knife is not fast enough. You nevertheless ought to try it out yourself.

Maybe you have seen the western *The Magnificent Seven*. If so, you may recall the famous knife throwing scene: cowboy Britt – played by James Coburn – takes out his revolver-armed opponent in the duel with an underhand throw as sure as death and over an estimated distance of about 32 feet (10 meters)! For this, he uses a light folder with a stiletto blade – very spectacular and also typical for Hollywood. It can be doubted that this technique really works under the given circumstances.

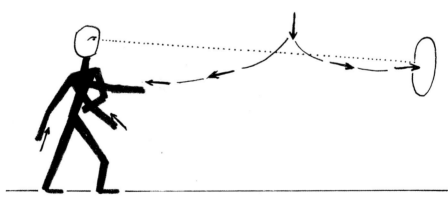

Shown schematically: underhand throw with half rotation.

Underhand throw from the flat hand: taking measure with the arm stretched backwards.

Position when letting go: the arm stays outstretched for the duration of the entire movement.

Pinch Grip for Folders

Actually, a folder is really too precious to throw, but maybe you still have an old piece somewhere for which it doesn't matter if it receives some damage. If this is the case, then grip it for throwing as shown below.

With the "pinch grip," hold the knife blade close to its tip between thumb and forefinger. The recommended distance for a rotation of about 400° is about 10 feet (3 meters). Caution: the knife rotates relatively fast. This is not easy to control. You will have to experiment a bit until you've got the hang of it.

Pinch grip: the blade is held between thumb and forefinger.

"NO SPIN" TECHNIQUE

For a few years, a magical word has been moving ghost-like amidst the knife throwing scene: "No spin"! This refers to a throwing technique with which the knife is thrown almost without any rotation – over all the varied distances. The German expression "Pfeilwurf" (literally: arrow throw) probably describes this technique best because the knife really moves tip forward during the entire flight to the target without ever flipping over once – just like an arrow.

The left image shows how to grip the knife for a throw: here, the forefinger lies outstretched below the guard on the back of the handle.

To the right you can see the motion sequence of letting go: the throwing hand and arm move like a whip with your wrist unlocked. Sometimes this is also called a "wave movement." While your hand moves forward, downward, and is opened, your forefinger glides along the handle back.

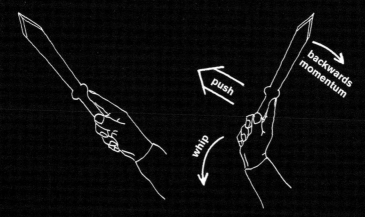

No spin technique in theory: the hand pushes the knife forward, at the same time it receives momentum against the direction of rotation.

This way the knife receives a backwards momentum which annihilates the rotation almost completely. At the same time, your throwing hand gives the knife a forceful push – a complex motion sequence which is not easy to master!

This throw quite often is done – especially over distances of about 16 feet (5 meters) and more – with a movement out of a lunging stance. It can be done with the knife over your head, at the side, or as an underhand throw. Ralph Thorn has described this technique extensively in his book (see Bibliography).

Taking measure: the handle is pinched between thumb and middle finger; the forefinger rests on the handle's back.

At the instant of letting go: the forefinger adds momentum against the direction of rotation.

WAYS OF CARRYING

Of course, it is your choice how and where you want to carry your throwing knives. Here, I introduce several possibilities.

Neck knife carried around the neck on a leather lanyard. The knife is kept in its sheath by frictional resistance.

Knife carried vertically in a thigh pocket.

On the belt, horizontally at the back.

In a double sheath at the shank.

Simple and traditional on the belt.

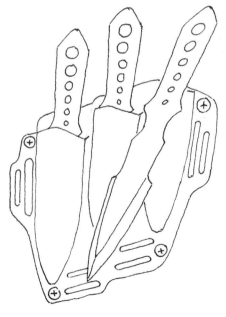

Set of three throwing knives in a shoulder harness (Shoulder Harness Triple Set of United Cutlery).

TRICK THROWS

After you have managed the basic throws, you can try various throws from different positions or from a movement:

- Running
- While seated
- While lying
- Backwards

Enhanced difficulty: throwing at the target while running.

The same technique as with a normal, standing throw: throwing while sitting.

More trying than it looks: throw from a lying position.

Aiming with difficulties: backwards throw from below.

KNIFE THROWING AS A TECHNIQUE FOR COMBAT AND SELF DEFENSE?

Sometimes the question poses itself whether knife throwing is suited as a technique for combat and self defense. Colonel Rex Applegate, the legendary U.S. Army expert on combat, writes on this in his book *Kill or Get Killed* (1961):

> *Knife throwing can be largely discounted as a practical method of combat. There are few individuals in the world who can pick up a knife, throw it at a moving object at an unknown distance, and hit a vital spot. In the main, knife throwing is an art relegated to vaudeville and stage, because, to throw a knife properly, the exact distance from the thrower to the target must be known. Since the knife turns end over end as it travels through the air, the thrower must know the exact distance. He must be able to control the number of turns the knife makes, so that it will hit the target point first.*
>
> *There are, indeed, methods of knife throwing, at close ranges, without the blade turning end over end in the air; but considering the movement of the target, varying distances, heavy clothing, and the fact that if you miss you are without a weapon, knife throwing is not practical as a means of attack.*

Michael D. Echanis, a renowned U.S. combat trainer, is more precise in his book *Knife Fighting, Knife Throwing for Combat* (Black Belt Books, 1978, p. 151f). He defines "close range" as 3 to 12 feet (about 1 to 3½ meters) and accordingly describes (knife) throwing techniques in combination with the Korean martial art Hwarangdo.

Blackie Collins and Ralph Thorn, two more U.S. American authors, also write about this topic in their books. While Collins gives deliberate consideration to the psychological aspects of knife throwing as a self defense technique, Thorn describes a combat technique developed by him that is based on especially prepared knives.

These are different approaches and views. Nevertheless, the fact is undisputed that knife throwing is very well suited to train the feel for movements, hand-eye coordination, and the ability to focus.

Template for Making a Throwing Knife

If you want to construct a throwing knife yourself, you can take this design made by the author as a template (just enlarge it to the desired size on a photocopying machine). The outline is based on the Escrima Fighting Knife (EFK) of the company Böker in Solingen, Germany.

For best results, use non-hardened sheet steel (*e.g.* V 4301) with a material thickness of a fifth of an inch (5 mm). In this case, the finished throwing knife, with a length of about 12 inches (30 cm), has almost exactly the ideal weight of 10½ ounces (300 grams).

The center of gravity is in the center of the knife and provides uniform rotations, regardless of throwing the knife by gripping its blade or its handle.

PART B: AXE THROWING

"Dog of the pale-faces!" he exclaimed in Iroquois, "go yell among the curs of your own evil hunting grounds!" The denunciation was accompanied by an appropriate action. Even while speaking his arm was lifted, and the tomahawk hurled. Luckily the loud tones of the speaker had drawn the eye of Deerslayer towards him, else would that moment have probably closed his career. So great was the dexterity with which this dangerous weapon was thrown, and so deadly the intent, that it would have riven the scull of the prisoner, had he not stretched forth an arm, and caught the handle in one of its turns, with a readiness quite as remarkable as the skill with which the missile had been hurled. The projectile force was so great, notwithstanding, that when Deerslayer's arm was arrested, his hand was raised above and behind his own head, and in the very attitude necessary to return the attack. It is not certain whether the circumstance of finding himself unexpectedly in this menacing posture and armed tempted the young man to retaliate, or whether sudden resentment overcame his forbearance and prudence. His eye kindled, however, and a small red spot appeared on each cheek, while he cast all his energy into the effort of his arm, and threw back the weapon at his assailant. The unexpectedness of this blow contributed to its success, the Panther neither raising an arm, nor bending his head to avoid it. The keen little axe struck the victim in a perpendicular line with the nose, directly between the eyes, literally braining him on the spot. Sallying forward, as the serpent darts at its enemy even while receiving its own death wound, this man of powerful frame fell his length into the open area formed by the circle, quivering in death. A common rush to his relief left the captive, in a single instant, quite without the crowd, and, willing to make one desperate effort for life, he bounded off with the activity of a deer. There was but a breathless instant, when the whole band, old and young, women and children, abandoning the lifeless body of the Panther where it lay, raised the yell of alarm and followed in pursuit.

Excerpt from:
James Fenimore Cooper: *The Deerslayer,* Gutenberg Edition, 2009, http://www.gutenberg.org/etext/3285

Maybe this story seems to be a bit bloodthirsty. But this and similar stories about the *Natives of North America* by J.F. Cooper, Karl May, and Fritz Steuben, fired the imagination of many generations. In movies, such as *The Last of* the *Mohicans* and *The Patriot,* they were turned into pictures.

Also think of the medieval warriors in Northern Europe. Not only the Vikings, but also the Saxons and Franks carried the battle axe instead of the sword – quite often also used as a throwing axe.

In the meantime, the martial weapon of long ago, surrounded by myths and sagas, has turned into a modern sports tool. The archaic desire to use it for hitting a target still remains.

Every now and then, you may hear that axe throwing is less demanding than knife throwing. This is only partially correct. Even as a beginner, you will learn relatively fast how to "plant" an axe into the wood with a single rotation. But as soon as precision is required or throws with more than one rotation from a greater distance, it becomes quickly obvious that the throwing axe pushes some throwers very close to their limit.

This is probably the reason why on the starting lists of the well-known contests for axe throwing a good deal fewer names show up than on those for knife-throwing contests. Maybe your name will soon show up in one of the starting lists for axe throwers?

Definition of Parts
Throwing Axe with Protective Sheath

The most important expressions with respect to throwing axes.

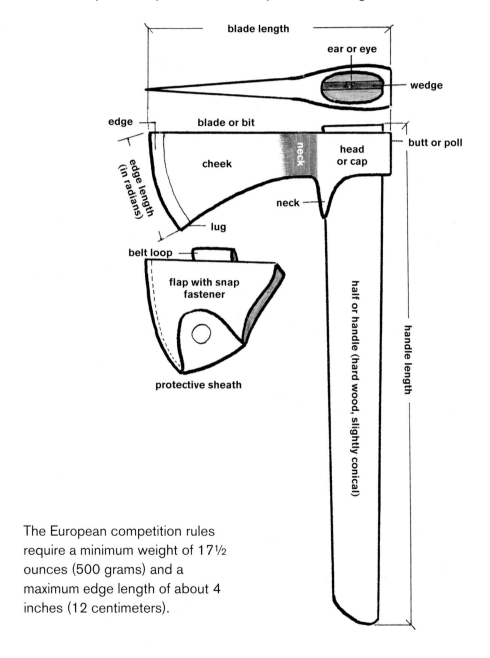

The European competition rules require a minimum weight of 17½ ounces (500 grams) and a maximum edge length of about 4 inches (12 centimeters).

DEFINITIONS

The expression "throwing axe" today is in general use for the corresponding sports tool. Here, it doesn't matter whether the tool in question really has similarities to an axe or rather looks like a hatchet or tomahawk. Despite their various shapes, the typical characteristics of these are unmistakable.

Axe

Axes were already used as weapons and tools by prehistoric humans. They are distinguished from hatchets by their smaller edge, longer handle (about 29 inches [75 centimeters]), and the higher weight (about 52 to 70 ounces [1,500 to 2,000 grams]). The handle of ash, beech, or maple wood is inserted into the rear end of the axe head, which is forged of steel. The handle can be straight or curved. Usually, axes are held with both hands. Their different shapes were developed to serve different purposes.

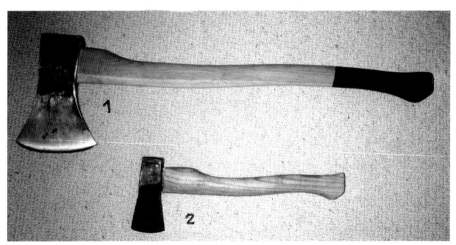

Axe and hatchet compared: above a modern axe for felling trees, below a hatchet for taking on camping trips.

Hatchet

Hatchets have been proved to exist since the Stone Age. At first they were hardly more than sharp-edged stones fixed to a club – weapons and tools at the same time. In contrast to axes, modern hatchets have distinctly less weight (about 28 ounces [800 grams]) and a shorter handle (about 15 inches [40 centimeters]). They are predominantly used as tools and are usually held with one hand. The most common form is a hand axe. The various shapes are a result of the requirements of different crafts, such as the axing of tree logs.

Tomahawk

The tomahawk (short: "hawk"), the battle axe of the Native Americans, is the most well-known throwing axe. The word "tamahaken" of the Algonquian language can be approximately translated as "cutting tool." A derivation of "otomahuk" ("to knock down") is also possible.

Reproduction of a pipe tomahawk used by the Plains tribes with blade cutout ("bleeding heart") and decorated handle.

Probably, the natives on the east coast of North America already came to know battle axes through contact with the Vikings during their exploration trips, while they themselves used club-like impact weapons. It was not before the 17th century that the tomahawk was introduced by the Europeans as a small steel axe (belt axe, hatchet). As an object for exchanging and trading, it soon became widespread. Since then, it is seen as a typical native weapon, but was also used by the white people as a weapon and tool. Different shapes were developed, such as the pipe tomahawk, which could also be used as a ritual peace pipe.

The tomahawk even influenced every-day language. In accordance with Native American tradition, we talk of "to take up the hatchet" when hostilities are started. The declaration of peace, in contrast, is described by the phrase "to bury the hatchet."

It is confirmed that the Native Americans not only used the tomahawk as a tool, a cutting weapon, and as a part of their ceremonies, but also used them very skillfully and accurately as a throwing weapon. Indeed, most modern sports throwing axes are very similar to Native American tomahawks.

Well-known shape: typical tomahawks with pointed spike opposite the blade.

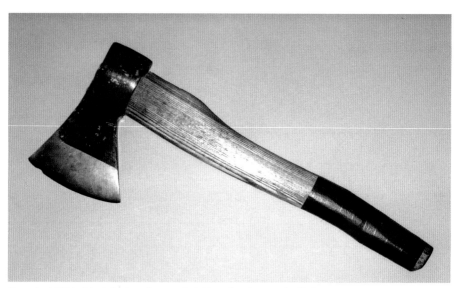

Reworked DIY-hatchet: the handle was straightened and covered with tape.

FOR A START...

...you don't need a real throwing axe. At first, a cheap hand axe from the DIY-store will do. But you absolutely have to change the lower part of the curved handle by straightening its butt. For this, first remove the surplus wood with a sharp knife. Then dress with a rasp and, finally, smooth the handle with abrasive paper.

Your self-made throwing axe should have a more or less straight handle in order for it to smoothly glide from your hand during the throw without your little finger catching somewhere. Such an unwanted effect could ruin your entire throw.

FROM HAND AXE TO THROWING AXE

With a bit of skill and the proper tools, you can turn this hand axe from the DIY-store – without much effort – into a throwing axe, which almost looks like a tomahawk.

First of all, detach the handle. Then remove the parts, which are shown as shaded areas on the drawing, with a disc grinder. You can also have this done at a locksmith's shop or metalworking business. The result not only enhances the optical impression, but also reduces the weight of the blade to about the recommended 17 ounces (500 grams).

Now the modified blade receives a new handle (see page 88 and 89) and is ready to go!

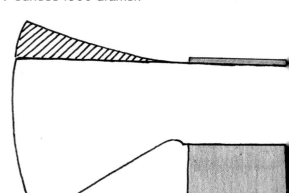

EDGE GRIND

The edge of a throwing axe can be ground into three different shapes. But only one of them is optimal.

Spherical Grind

With this grind, the sides of the edge have a radius bulging to the outside (convex). Although this edge is stable, it is less suited for a throwing axe, because it doesn't penetrate deeply when it hits the wooden target. If the wood is hard, it may even happen that a perfect throw doesn't stick, but bounces back. During the contest, this means an annoying loss of points.

Hollow Grind

Here, the sides of the edge are curved inwards (concave). This type of grind, too, is not recommended. Although the tapered edge will in any case penetrate deeply even in hard wood, it is so delicate that nicks and fractures can hardly be avoided.

Flat Grind

Here, the sides of the edge form an acute angle. This is the optimal edge shape for a throwing axe. It guarantees sufficient stability, will always penetrate deep enough into the wood, and will reliably stick in the target.

IT IS VERY SIMPLE!

Here is a guide for tomahawk throwing from an U.S. publication that explains the entire issue in an easy-to-understand way.

Step 1: You need a good hawk for throwing.

Step 2: Obtain something that you can use as a target. A section from the end of a tree log with a thickness of about one foot is suitable.

Step 3: Stand with your back against the section and move about six steps forward. Then turn around and face the target.

Step 4: Hold the tomahawk at the base of its handle and throw it, like a pitcher in baseball.

If you don't hit the target this way, step a bit forward or move slightly farther away.

P. S. If you hold the handle close to its base and point in the direction you want to throw, the hawk will find the target somehow.

Fig. 3

HOLDING THE AXE

Hold the handle of your throwing axe close to its base – in a similar way to holding a hammer (left photo). But don't hold on too hard, because the handle should glide from your hand during the throw!

If you put your thumb onto the handle instead (right photo), you will realize that it is easier to guide the throwing axe cleanly in the direction of throw this way. Besides this, the rotation is also slowed down distinctly. With respect to the distance to the target, the difference is about 3 feet (1 meter).

This means, if you are able to hit the target with two rotations from a distance of about 23 feet (7 meters) using a normal hammer grip, you should be successful from a distance of 26 feet (8 meters) with the thumb on top. Here, the same maxim holds: just try!

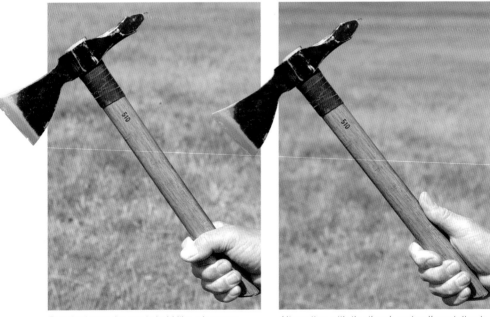

Standard grip: the axe is held like a hammer.

Alternative: with the thumb on top the rotation is slowed down.

MOTION SEQUENCE

These images make clear that the individual phases of the motion sequence during axe throwing are basically not different from those we reviewed for knife throwing.

The individual phases of the motion sequence from left to right: taking measure, bringing your arm back, throwing, following through.

"Taking measure": the throwing arm is outstretched.

"Bringing your arm back": The body weight is mostly on your left foot.

"Throwing": The upper torso is bent forward; the arm is outstretched.

"Following through": the downwards movement is continued...

... until the throwing hand rests on the left knee.

A BIT OF PHYSICS*

The trajectory of a throwing axe is determined by:

- the initial velocity A (which results from the applied force)
- the angle at which the axe is thrown (alpha)
- the rotation R
- the earth's gravitational pull E
- the drag L

From the interaction of these forces, there results the parabolic trajectory P with the ascending branch P1 and the descending branch P2, *i.e.,* a parabolic curve starting at the thrower's hand H and ending at the target Z.

With increasing distance to the target, you have to increase the throwing angle and/or the used force.

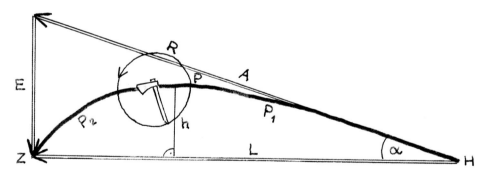

Diagram of forces: The gravity E pulls the axe down. The distance it flies depends on the angle a at throwing and the initial velocity A.

*On purpose, the generally used symbols for the various physical quantities were not used here.

HALF A ROTATION

If you want to make the throw with half a rotation, you have to hold the throwing axe in your hand in such a way that its edge faces backwards. As a result, it will stick in the target, as can be seen in this picture, with the handle facing upwards. Of course, the same goes for throws with one and a half, two and a half, or three and a half rotations.

This also works: after a throw with half a rotation, the axe handle faces upwards.

CENTER OF GRAVITY AND ROTATION

For most throwing axes, the center of gravity lies about 1 to 3 inches (3-7 centimeters) below the head. Its exact location depends on the weight of the axe head, as well as on the qualities and length of the handle.

Checking the center of gravity: the center of rotation usually can be found just behind the axe's head.

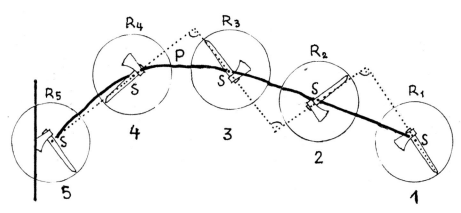

Throw from 13 feet (4 meters) distance with one rotation

1. Throwing axe leaves the hand
2. First quarter of the rotation (90°)
3. Half rotation (180°)
4. Third quarter of the rotation (270°)

5. Rotation completed/throwing axe hits the target (360°)
S= center of gravity
R1–R5= rotational radii
P= throwing parabola

HANDLE LENGTH

On the left photo at the bottom of this page you can see that the handle length apparently has an influence on how the axe sticks in the target. All three throws were made from a distance of about 13 feet (4 meters) and with one rotation. Special emphasis was put on a clean execution – especially when letting go of the axe.

The trapper axe in the center (about 24 ounces/16 inches [700 grams/41 centimeters]) sticks in the target in such a way that the handle is almost vertical. This means it rotated more or less exactly 360°. The smaller hatchet in front (about 20 ounces/12 inches [575 grams/33 centimeters]), in contrast, did a rotation of about 400°, while the small hand axe in the background with the red blade (about 15 ounces/11 inches [450 grams/30 centimeters]) rotated around 450° approximately.

The explanation is obvious: a lightweight axe with short handle rotates faster than a heavy axe with long handle. Furthermore, a light axe with a small handle rotates more often over a given distance than a heavier one with a long handle. This can be used: if you hold the handle at about half of its entire length, you can accelerate its rotation.

Same distance, different angles: the length of the handle affects the rotation.

Little trick: if you hold the handle "short," the axe rotates faster.

ATTACHING THE HANDLE

The handle of an axe has to endure a lot, especially if it bounces against the target during a miss. In this case, the handle often breaks and the broken part has to be replaced. Suitable parts for replacement are not frequently available. At best, you'll find a hammer handle at the DIY-store, which probably has to be finished.

But you can also produce a handle yourself: obtain a piece of well-matured hard wood (*e.g.* ash or maple), about 15¾ inches (40 centimeters) in length and with a rectangular cross-section of a little over an inch by just under an inch (3.5 x 2.0 centimeters). Of course, the dimensions depend on the size of the eye of your throwing axe.

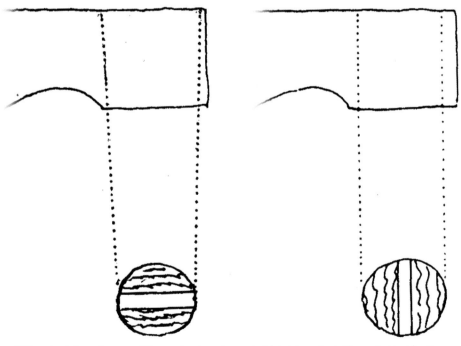

Different solutions: the eye of the axe head can be conical (sketch on the left) or cylindrical (on the right). The handle is held more reliably, if the eye is conical.

Work on this piece of wood first with a sharp knife, then with a rasp and a file, until all corners are smoothed and the finished handle fits flush into the eye. This is precision work. While shaping, you have to take into account whether the eye is conical or cylindrical (see sketch on the left side, page 88) and whether it is oval or circular. A handle with an oval cross-section which is tapered towards the butt lies especially well in the hand.

Now the handle is smoothed with abrasive paper and finally varnished with linseed oil or lacquer. When the coating has dried, with a saw you cut a slit from above into the part of the handle which will receive the eye later on. Then you put the handle into the eye and secure it with a fitting wedge. It is hammered into the slit from above. In addition, it can be fixed with wood glue. Here, it is up to you, whether you put the wedge across or in the direction of the blade. But it should always be parallel to the wood grain.

If the eye is shaped conically, the wedging is superfluous because the handle is held in the eye due to its being jammed there. In case the connection between handle and blade becomes loose, it helps to put the axe in water for a couple of minutes to soak the wood.

Always take care that handle and blade are connected firmly!

THROWING AXE TYPES

Classic Models

Throwing axes, too, come in many different variants – although the choice is not as large as with throwing knives. Here, I want to introduce just a few typical examples. Only after trying out several different models, should you decide on the one you feel most comfortable with. Of course, here the optical impression also comes into play. Sometimes it may be necessary to modify a throwing axe in a way to better fit your requirements.

Elegant shape: so-called French trade axe with hammer head.

Early form: hand-forged Viking axe (beard axe), robust and shapely with a distinctive beard. The edge length of this axe is not compliant with the rules for competitions.

Typical examples: big and small throwing axe with leather wrapping in the frontal area.

Throwing hatchet "Wildmark": This hatchet with a die-forged blade, developed by Willy Albicker (Wildmark-Versand), allows very precise throws. The blade is shaped like that of a "Franziska" (see page 94) and has a distinctive "nose."

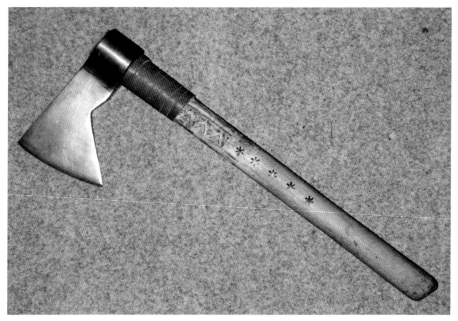

Robust trapper axe: sometimes these models, whose back of the head is not shaped in any way, are named "squaw axe."

Throwing axe "Trail Hawk": this robust and effective axe with hammer head is made in Taiwan for the company ATC. The company Cold Steel, too, has a wide variety of throwing axes on offer.

Pirate axe: this massive and artistic piece of forging with twisted area between blade and head was made according to a historical piece of the 17th century.

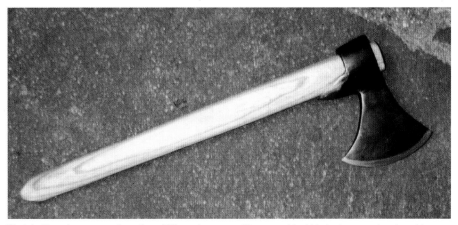

Virginia throwing axe: replica of an 18th century axe with symmetrical blade, hammer head, and lug. The edge is ground spherically.

Throwing axes from a single piece of steel: with these models, the feared handle fractures are almost impossible. The cutouts in head and handle reduce the weight.

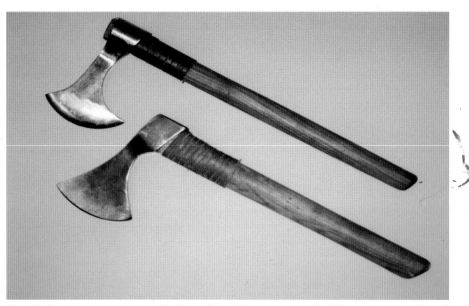

Frankish throwing axes: replicas of the "Franziska," which was used by Frankish warriors in the 3rd and 4th centuries. The pronounced "nose" enables the axe to stick in a vertical target, even if the handle is already horizontally oriented.

Tactical Tomahawks

More than fifty years ago, the former U.S. Marine Peter LaGana designed his "fighting tomahawk" based on his experience during the Second World War. It was not only meant as a handy tool, but also as a weapon in close combat. LaGana improved his tomahawk several times and finally founded the American Tomahawk Company (ATC).

During the Vietnam War, he primarily delivered his tomahawks to the soldiers on duty there. These so-called Vietnam tomahawks (VTAC) are still in military use today, almost unchanged. Only the wooden handle was replaced by one made of acetyl for the more recent models. Nevertheless, the VTAC was never an official weapon of the U.S. armed forces. The soldiers buy them at their own expense and carry them as part of their equipment while on duty in foreign countries.

The VTAC was and still is an archetype for other makers. The company SOG Specialty Knives & Tools, for example, not only offers an exact replica, but, under the name "Fusion," also a new model whose similarity to the Vietnam tomahawk is quite obvious. The holes in the blade reduce weight. But the original hardwood handle was weak due to the unusual connection to the head (strap and jacket). Quite often, the handle was

LaGana's Vietnam tomahawk: modern ATC-version with acetyl handle (24 ounces/14 inches [675 grams/36 centimeters]). The handle is held reliably in the eye by means of an Allen screw set vertically in the handle's head.

Improved version: SOG "Fusion" tomahawk with plastic material handle.

already broken off due to the rotational forces which occur at impact. Thus, SOG replaced the handle with one of plastic material so the problem no longer occurs. This way, a tomahawk was created that can be thrown well, is robust, and elegant, too.

Not Recommended

From the point of view of a sporty thrower, the following criteria are considered negative for a throwing axe:

• An extravagant design puts emphasis on optics, not performance.
• Strongly profiled handles hamper letting go without adding torque.
• Blades with more than a single edge can falsify the appearance of hits and thus cost you precious points during competitions.

Be critical and don't let yourself be deceived by sales-promotional effects!

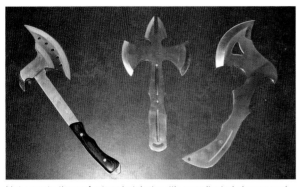

Not easy to throw: fantasy hatchets with complicated shapes and multiple edges.

Unfavorable: camping hatchets with curved handle.

Important extra: protective covers for the axe blade.

PROTECTIVE COVER AND SHEATH

The sharp edge of your axe represents a certain risk for injuries. Because of this, the edge should be covered when the axe is not in use. Either this should be done by means of a protective cover, which covers the edge and surrounds part of the blade, or by means of a sheath surrounding the entire blade and can be carried on the belt, if needed.

THROWING DOUBLE AXES

Double axes are heavy throwing axes with a long handle, a mandatory minimum weight of 40 ounces (1134 grams) and a minimum handle length of 24 inches (61 centimeters). It has two symmetrical blades, with edges that are required to be no longer than 6 inches (152 millimeters) each. For taking aim, it is guided quite far behind your back with both hands and then thrown towards the target from above your head.

Because of its high weight and long handle, the axe rotates relatively slowly on its way through the air. Thus, it hits the target from the predetermined distance of 20 feet (6.1 meters) after one full rotation. Here, hits are only counted if the axe sticks in the target with its front edge while the handle faces downwards.

The target disc has a center (value 5 points) and four rings (value 1 to 4 points). Its diameter is about 3 feet (1 meter). In case the axe cuts two lines, the higher value is counted.

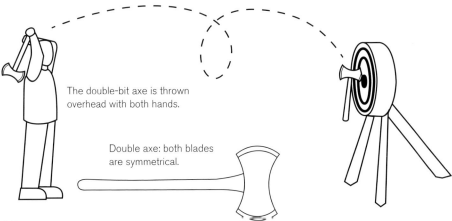

The double-bit axe is thrown overhead with both hands.

Double axe: both blades are symmetrical.

PART C: APPENDIX

Legal Aspects

Even though it may sound trivial, it will be important for anyone undertaking this sport to research and then practice the laws for their respective locations, whether that be country, or states/municipalities within a country, or other locals.

Knives not classified as forbidden objects (such as balisongs and push daggers in Germany) can be bought and owned, but there are specifics that should be understood legally. Throwing knives are usually seen as sports tools, however, that may not preclude them from being considered as concealed weapons if you carry them on your person in some places. An example in the United States would be that the state of Texas outlaws illegal knives, and this is described as "any hand instrument that is designed to either cut, or stab another person by being thrown." Laws there further define a knife as "any bladed hand instrument capable of inflicting serious damage, injury or death either through cutting or stabbing." It stands to reason that the laws must be closely studied. Another example: the state of Florida, while not seeing throwing knives as illegal, does have specific rules regarding how and what is carried on one's person.

Legal aspects also do not stop at local or state levels in America. The U.S. Federal Government, too, has laws prohibiting people from transporting knives. There are specific descriptions that apply in this legislation.

Read more about this at the following websites:
www.ehow.com/list_6620857_laws-throwing-knives.html
www.ehow.com/list_6620857_laws-throwing-knives.html
www.knifeup.com

Unclear in a similar way is the position with respect to throwing axes. They, too, are firstly tools or sports utensils and not cut and thrust weapons. But is a tomahawk not also a battle axe? At least for Karl May and J.F. Cooper! And weren't the Vietnam tomahawks also used as feared weapons for close combat? What is the intended purpose of a "tactical tomahawk"? Such questions show how differently our throwing tools may be assessed and the consequences we may face as a result.

Research thoroughly for the laws that will affect your particular situation.

Strongly recommended: Stowing and transporting the throwing objects in a lockable hard-top case.

Thrower Meetings and Contests

Since 2000, the websites www.messerwerfen.de and www.axethrowing.de have been online. These were the trigger for the first thrower meetings in Germany, which already centered on knife and axe throwing contests. Besides regional contests, the "Großes Werfertreffen" (Great Throwing Competition) was established, which at first was held several times in the state of Brandenburg, Germany. Later on it was performed each year as "European Throwing Competition" at different places in Germany, France, Italy and the Czech Republic.

During one of these throwing competitions, in 2003, 14 founding members christened the "European Throwing Club Flying Blades (Eurothrowers)". This society – with an ever increasing number of members – has as a goal to create a pan-European network for knife and axe throwing, to make it popular, and to help with organizing contests.

Today throwers from many European countries and overseas are part of it. Thus the 10th European meeting of throwers in Rome in September 2010 could officially be conducted as the first European championship in knife and axe throwing. Binding rules for international competitions in Europe were finalized as well.

As standard disciplines, these rules list throwing contests from a distance of three meters, five meters, and seven meters with the knife and from a distance of four and seven meters with the axe. The participants conduct twenty-one throws, each towards a target disc with five rings and a diameter of fifty centimeters. Here, precision is required. In addition, there are distance contests with knife and axe that require hits from as large a distance as possible.

In contrast to other European countries, there are no local knife and axe throwing societies in Germany. Nevertheless, in the regions of Schleswig-Holstein, Lower Bavaria, Frankfurt, and the Black Forest, interest groups have been founded which practice throwing double-bit axes.

In 2014, the First Knife and Axe Throwing World Championships took place at Callac/France. There were 150 throwers from 11 countries all over the world. Besides the usual standards, new disciplines were invented, such as speed throwing, instinctive throwing from unknown distances with half or no spin, silhouette throwing, fast draw duelling, walk back precision, and others

In the United States, the American Knife Throwers Alliance was founded in 1971 to provide assistance and guidelines for those wanting to become involved in this competitive sport within local areas around the country. This club recognizes knife throwing as not only a sport, but also as a hobby or recreational activity and thus supports members in a variety of these venues. (www.akta-usa.com)

The International Knife Throwers Hall of Fame, located in Austin, Texas, was established in 2003 to honor knife throwers, educate the public about throwing, and to preserve knife throwing as part of America's culture (www.ikthof.com). Texas has been recognized as having the largest concentration of knife throwers in the nation.

The United States has a varied complement of throwing clubs that provide members such connections as, for example, inclusion in a martial arts school program in Montgomery, Alabama (Feathers and Steel) and a team club (Bakido Knife Throwing Club) in Austin, Texas. There, of course, are the traditional clubs located throughout the country, such as the Carolina Bladeslingers in North Carolina, the Highland Hurlers in Frazier Park, California, the Pine Splitters in Pennsylvania, and others (i.e., Pacific, Rocky Mountains, Louisiana, and other states).

Varied research and communications websites list throwing events (times, locations, requirements) held throughout the country (for example, The Great Throwzini at www.throwzini.com/events.html) and it is usual to find information like this at all local club websites, or other contact venues.

Target for a Tree Disc on Tripod

1. 2 square timbers: 2¾ inches x 1½ inches x 67 inches (7 cm x 4 cm x 170 cm)

2. support: 2¾ inches x 1½ inches x 65 inches (7 cm x 4 cm x 165 cm)

3. trapezoidal connector (thickness 1 inch [3 cm])

4. trapezoidal connector (thickness 1 inch [3 cm])

5. 2 side pieces

6. hinge

7. chipboard screws 2¼ inches (6 cm) (20 items)

8. chipboard screws 1 inch (3 cm) (10 items)

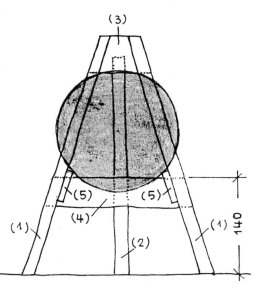

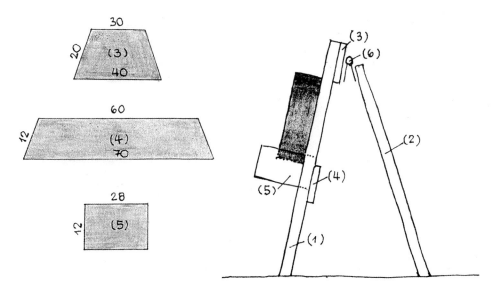

RESOURCES

Internet Addresses

Here you find a selection of relevant addresses which provide you with further information on the topic of knife and axe throwing:

www.messerwerfen.de

www.axtwerfen.de

www.messerpete.de

www.eurothrowers.org

www.hacklwerfa.de

www.akta-usa.com

www.throwzini.com

www.jackdagger.com

www.stickingpoint.com

www.combatknifethrowing.com

www.alca68.free.fr

www.lancercouteaux.info

www.maitrelanceur.info

www.lanciatori.virtuale.org

Bibliography

Applegate, *Rex. Kill or Get Killed*, The Military Service Publishing Company. Harrisburg PS 1961

Bär, Markus. *Sportliches Messerwerfen*, Verlag Weinmann. Berlin 1989

Berg, Elisabet. *Das Buch der Äxte, Erikson & Gullberg*. Stockholm 1996

Böll, Heinrich. Der Mann mit den Messern, in Der neue Robinson. Texte Band 2, CC Buchners Verlag, Hamburg 1961

Bothe, Carsten. *Das Messerbuch, Venatus Verlags GmbH Braunschweig 1997*

Buerlein, Robert A. *Allied Military Fighting Knives and the Men who Made Them Famous*. The American Historical Foundation, Richmond VA 1961

Catania, Philippe. *Du Lancer de Couteau,* self published, n. d.

Collins, Blackie. *Knife Throwing*, Knife World Publications, Knoxville TN, n. d.

Echanis, Michael D. *Knife Fighting, Knife Throwing for Combat*. Black Belt Books, n. d.

Ettig, Wolfgang. *Messerwerfen als Sport und Hobby*. Verlag W. Ettig, Bad Homburg 1989

Grant, David. *Tomahawks – Traditional to Tactical*. Paladin Press, Boulder CO, 2007

Gurstelle, William. *Absinthe and Flamethrowers: Ruminations on the Art of Living Dangerously*, Chicago Review Press, Chicago IL 2009

Heavrin, Charles A.. *The Axe and Man*. The Astral Press, Mendham NJ 1998

Hibben, Gil. *The Complete Gil Hibben Knife Throwing Guide*. United Cutlery Corp., Sevierville TN 1994

Lecoeur, Gerard. *Le Couteau de Lancer*. Edition Crepin-Leblond 1998

Madden, James W. *The Art of Throwing Weapons*. Paladin Press, Boulder CO 1991

Marinas, Amante P. *Pananandata Guide to Knife Throwing*. United Cutlery Corp., Sevierville TN 1999

McEvoy, Harry K. *Knife Throwing in the Professional Style*. The Tru-Bal Company, Grand Rapids 1969; *Knife Throwing*. Charles E. Tuttle Company, Rutland VT 1980; "Tale of the Tomahawk." in: *Knife World*, Knoxville TN 1980; *Knife and Tomahawk Throwing*. Charles E. Tuttle Company, Rutland VT 1988; *Knife and Tomahawk Throwing*. Knife World Publications, Knoxville TN n. d.

Millhauser, Steven. *The Knife Thrower and Other Stories*. Phoenix, London 1999

Petersen, Harold L. *American Indian Tomahawks*. Heye Foundation, Glückstadt 1971

Thorn, Ralph. *Combat Knife Throwing*. Loompanics Unlimited, Port Townsend 2002